CHILDREN 92 LEIV EIRIKSSON
   2014
Bankston, John
Leif Erikson

07/31/2013

JUNIOR
BIOGRAPHY
FROM
ANCIENT
CIVILIZATIONS

LEIF ERIKSON

JOHN BANKSTON

Mitchell Lane
PUBLISHERS

P.O. Box 196
Hockessin, Delaware 19707

JUNIOR BIOGRAPHY FROM
ANCIENT CIVILIZATIONS

Alexander the Great • Archimedes
Augustus Caesar • Confucius • Genghis Khan
Homer • Leif Erikson • Marco Polo
Nero • Socrates

Copyright © 2014 by Mitchell Lane Publishers

Printing   1   2   3   4   5   6   7   8   9

ABOUT THE AUTHOR: Born in Boston,
Massachusetts, John Bankston began writing
articles while still a teenager. Since then,
over two hundred of his articles have been
published in magazines and newspapers
across the country, including travel articles
in *The Tallahassee Democrat, The Orlando
Sentinel* and *The Tallahassean.* He is the
author of over eighty books for young adults,
including biographies of scientist Stephen
Hawking, author F. Scott Fitzgerald and actor
Jodi Foster.

PUBLISHER'S NOTE: The facts on which the story
in this book is based have been thoroughly
researched. Documentation of such research
can be found on pages 44–45. While every
possible effort has been made to ensure
accuracy, the publisher will not assume
liability for damages caused by inaccuracies
in the data, and makes no warranty on the
accuracy of the information contained herein.

Library of Congress
Cataloging-in-Publication Data

Bankston, John, 1974–
 Leif Erikson / by John Bankston.
    pages cm. — (Junior biography from
ancient civilizations)
 Includes bibliographical references and index.
 ISBN 978-1-61228-430-9 (library bound)
 1. Leiv Eiriksson, –approximately 1020—Juvenile
literature. 2. Explorers—America—Biography—
Juvenile literature. 3. Explorers—Scandinavia—
Biography—Juvenile literature. 4. America—
Discovery and exploration—Norse—Juvenile
literature. 5. Vikings—Juvenile literature. I. Title.
 E105.L47B36 2013
 970.01'3092—dc23
 [B]
                                        2013012556

eBook ISBN: 9781612284965

                                        PLB

CONTENTS

Phonetic pronunciations of words in **bold**
can be found on page 46.

One of the world's most famous sailors and explorers, Viking Leif Erikson is honored with a statue outside the Mariners' Museum in Newport News, Virginia.

Bjarni Herjólfsson* never forgot the forest. He saw the tree-lined shore from the deck of the ship he commanded after it had become lost. Ten years later, he described it to an eagerly listening teenager named **Leif** Erikson. The two of them were in Greenland, an island covered by snow and frost that was far more white than green. When Leif heard Bjarni's vivid descriptions of the forest, he wanted to go there.

Though he was just 15, Leif Erikson was already trained in combat and in navigation. He could sail a ship and command groups of fighting men. He knew he was ready to sail toward unexplored lands.

Ten years earlier, about 985, Leif's family had settled in Greenland. At almost the same time, Bjarni Herjólfsson had sailed from Norway. He'd planned to visit his father, who lived near Leif's family. Instead, Bjarni's ship became lost in thick fog. When it finally

*For pronunciations of words in **bold**, see page 46.

emerged, Bjarni saw an unfamiliar shoreline. His exhausted crew begged him to land. Bjarni refused.

Bjarni enjoyed talking about his adventures. Unlike Leif, he was not interested in exploration. He was only interested in trading. Bjarni took goods from Greenland and Iceland like cattle, goats and valuable walrus tusks. He loaded them onto a 50-foot trading ship called a **knorr** and headed east to Norway. There he traded for gold and silver.

Leif's father was a powerful, successful leader named Erik the Red. He'd settled Greenland when Leif was a small boy. Erik transformed the barren landscape into a thriving community that now was home to more than 2,000 people.

Leif wanted to explore the land Bjarni described. If he succeeded, he could move out from under his father's shadow. Harvesting timber and selling it in Greenland could make Leif as rich and powerful as his father.

Leif Erikson, his father, and Bjarni were Vikings. Vikings first settled in Scandinavia. Today this is the area where Denmark, Sweden and Norway are located. Over a thousand years ago, Scandinavia was made up of small regions ruled by kings, chiefs, and jarls, or earls. Below these royals, "housekarls" were like the king's bodyguards. "Stallers" took care of horses. Most Vikings were "freemen," or "bondi." They owned land or worked as traders and merchants. Freemen grew crops or raised animals, often with the help of slaves called "thralls." Thralls were often men and women captured in battle. They were the lowest class in Viking society. When a wealthy landowner died, his thralls often joined him in the grave—even if they were still alive!

Although Vikings "sternly taught their children that each man's class was a decree of the Gods,"[1] some freemen became chiefs by getting more land and riches. As they sought more land and opportunities, some left Scandinavian countries for Iceland and Greenland. Other Vikings became rich by going on raids.

What today is known as the Age of the Vikings began in 793 when Vikings attacked the British town of **Lindisfarne**. A letter sent to King **Aethelred** of Northumbria described the attack: "Such a voyage was not thought possible. The church of St. Cuthbert is splattered with the blood of the priests . . . exposed to the plundering of the pagans."[2]

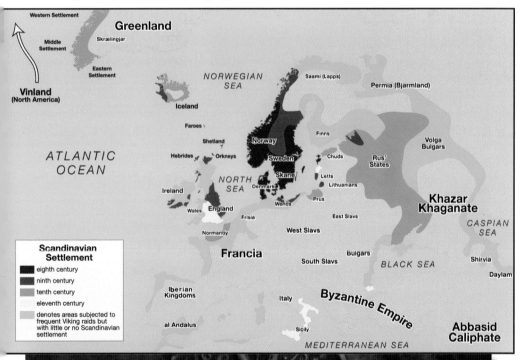

As this map of Scandinavian settlements illustrates, by the 11th century, Vikings had settled in territories across Europe and were pushing far into the Atlantic Ocean. North America, or Vinland to the Vikings, lies northwest of the map's borders.

For hundreds of years, Vikings attacked towns and churches across Europe. They even reached Russia. The Vikings became known as a dangerous, warring people. Popular stories dating back to more than one thousand years ago describe many of the Vikings' deadly raids.

"The Landing of the Vikings," an illustration by Arthur C. Michael, in *This Country of Ours: The Story of the United States* by H.E. Marshall.

These tales were often written by the victims. They made the Vikings seem brutal and heartless. During The Age of the Vikings, entire villages were burned to the ground and men, women, and children were killed.

By the time that Leif was born, these raids were starting to taper off. As the population of Vikings continued to increase, they needed new places to settle. They had already used up most of the arable land in Norway. They began colonizing islands such as the **Faeroes**, the **Hebrides**, and Iceland. With those sites rapidly filling up, they were always on the lookout for new settlement sites. As a result of that search, Leif Erikson reached North America 500 years before Christopher Columbus.

Viking Longships

From the time the Vikings first settled in Scandinavia, boats were an important part of their lives. With Scandinavia's challenging interior and much of the coastline dotted by fjords, the easiest way to get around was by boat.

The most famous Viking vessels were called longships. The front of the longship, or the prow, was curved upward. Prows were often carved with fierce-looking dragons. Because they often traveled across stormy seas, the ships were well-built. After the keel was attached, the boat was built up plank by plank. Then the shipwright added the rest of what was needed.

Longships were sleek and fast, so the Vikings could surprise their enemies. They also had a very shallow draft, so they could come right up to the shore. The heavily armed Vikings swarmed out and quickly attacked.

Longships had a single sail to propel them over long distances. For short bursts, the men sat on chests and pulled oars that were nearly 20 feet long.

Viking saw their longships as the means to gain riches and a reward in the afterlife. Some wealthy Vikings were even buried in their ships.

This example of a longship rests in Leif Erikson Park in Duluth, Minnesota.

Located beside Lake Superior, the wooden boat is the same size as the one used by Erikson and other Vikings.

Given to fiery fits of temper, Erik the Red earned his name for the color of his hair and his rages. His statue peers at visitors to the Stave Church, inside the Norway Pavilion at Florida's Epcot Center.

CHAPTER 2
Punishing Voyages

The ship was ready to sail when the small boy begged his father to take him along. His father refused. Leif Erikson was barely a toddler and his dad was leaving. He would be gone for at least three years. He might never come back.

Leif Erikson's dad was being banished. That meant he would live away from his family and his home. Banishment was like a prison sentence. *The Book of the Icelanders* explains that "Many chieftains were convicted or exiled for manslaughter [murder] or assault."[1]

Leif's father, Erik **Thorvaldson**, was called "Erik the Red." He earned the nickname for his bright red hair and beard. He also owned a red-hot temper. Banishment ran in the family. Erik's father, **Thorvald Aswaldson**, had fled to Iceland after he was banished from Norway for murder. Now Erik the Red was being forced to leave Iceland for the same reason.

Iceland is located near the very top of a globe, just below the Arctic Circle. It is so far north that there are days during the summer when the sun never completely sets!

Three hundred miles across, and 190 miles from north to south, it lies one week's sail from Norway. According to legend, it was first discovered by a Viking named Naddod around 860. Despite its location so far north, an ocean current called the North Atlantic Drift makes the island warmer than most other places near the Arctic Circle. It also benefited from a period called the Medieval Warm Period, which lasted for about 400 years between 800 and 1200.

Large, slow-moving sheets of ice called glaciers prevented early explorers from settling in parts of the island. Other areas were dangerous because Iceland is home to about 130 volcanoes. Some are still active.

The western coast offered numerous places for Vikings to settle. Leif's family lived at the head of a small bay near where the village of **Budardalur** is today. Scholars believe he was born there around 980. In 982 or 983 his father faced banishment.

The Vikings did not have formal courts. Instead they set up local councils, called "Things." In Iceland, each of the four provinces had its own Thing. They joined together to form an Althing, similar to the U.S. Congress. Because it was made up of landowners and merchants who represented their neighbors, it is considered to be the world's first example of representative democracy.

The Althing decided punishments and was more powerful than a village chief or king. Instead of prison or execution, people convicted of serious crimes were banished.

Erik the Red first got in trouble in the 980s after he killed his neighbor, **Eyjolf** Saver, and another man named **Hrafn** the Dueler. Dueling is a formal fight, often to the death, to settle differences. Hrafn died living up to his name.

Eyjolf's relatives went before the Althing. Erik the Red was sentenced to outlawry. He had to leave Iceland and stay away for three years. Before then, he was allowed to live on the island of Eyxney. There Eyjolf's relatives were not allowed to kill him.

On Eyxney, Erik the Red got into another fight with a neighbor. Erik killed this neighbor as well.

Perhaps realizing how poorly Erik got along with his neighbors, the Althing sentenced him to full outlawry. This meant anywhere on Iceland the man's relatives would not be punished for killing Erik the Red. An Icelander could even kill Erik in Norway.

The only way Erik could be safe was to go somewhere he couldn't be attacked. Instead of heading east toward Norway, he headed west to an area first seen by a Viking named **Gunnbjorn Ulfsson**. Like Bjarni Herjólfsson, Gunnbjorn Ulfsson got lost leaving Norway. He was headed to Iceland sometime around 900, but storms blew him off his intended course. He saw some small unfamiliar islands, which he named Gunnbjorn's skerries.

By the time Erik the Red was banished, Iceland was crowded—at least too crowded for Erik. He turned his punishment into opportunity. Along with his crew, he sailed some three hundred miles from Iceland, hoping to find Gunnbjorn's skerries. He had a pretty good idea of where to look. A few years earlier, a fellow Icelander named **Snæbjörn Galti** had sailed there, hoping to establish a colony. He failed and died in the effort.

13

Encountering a frozen wasteland, Erik the Red was unhappy with what he first saw from the bow of a Viking longboat in 982. Despite this, he soon settled there and named it "Greenland."

At first, Erik was unhappy. Gunnbjorn's skerries was a frozen wasteland. Along the coast, he could see glaciers. Erik and his men continued on, sailing around the southern tip of Greenland. They reached the western coast, which was lined with fjords. Beside the fjords were pastures. There was enough land for the Vikings to raise animals and farm.

For the next three years, Erik the Red explored. He traveled over one thousand miles along the region.

In Iceland, Erik's friends and family assumed he'd died. Instead, nearly four years after leaving, Erik returned. He was a hero with plans for a new settlement.

Today houses are sometimes sold by people who make them sound better than they really are. Rundown homes might be called "fixer-uppers." A tiny, cramped cottage could be called "cozy." Erik the Red apparently did something similar. He believed that if potential settlers focused on the island's frozen east coast, they almost certainly wouldn't want to move there. To make his discovery sound more attractive, Erik the Red gave it a name to make it more appealing. As *The Saga of Erik the Red* explains, "In the summer [Erik] went to live in the land which he had discovered, and which he called Greenland, 'Because,' said he, 'men will desire much the more to go there if the land has a good name.' "[2] Soon he would be bringing hundreds of settlers into the land he'd named.

For some Vikings, getting lost meant finding unknown lands. For others, getting lost meant death in the unforgiving ocean.

When they first left Scandinavia on raids, Vikings stayed within sight of land. They memorized the natural features of the landscape: cliffs and mountains, bays and rivers.

In the Atlantic Ocean, Vikings used seagulls to let them know when they were close to shore. Cloud formations and whale sightings suggested the same thing. By watching the setting or rising sun, a Viking could determine west and east. At night the North Star offered guidance as it had for countless other seafarers.

Vikings also used mechanical devices to help determine their location. Although some authorities suggest they used a crude compass, there is no convincing evidence. They did, however, use a sun shadow board at noon each day to see if they were on the correct course. The board had several circles and a large stick which cast shadows upon the board. They looked at the location of the shadow the stick cast in relation to the circles to figure

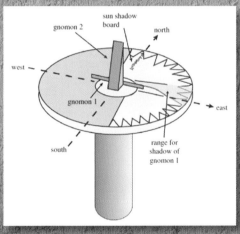

This compass dial is a combination of the Viking sun shadow board and a sun-compass.

out where they were in terms of north or south. This is often called "latitude sailing," and it let them know if they were too far north or south, or heading exactly where they wanted to go.

After Erik the Red returned to Iceland, he spoke to Viking leaders and others about a place he believed was perfect for new settlements: Greenland.

CHAPTER 3
Life in a Harsh Land

Leif was around six years old when he boarded one of the 25 ships leaving Iceland for Greenland. As many as 1,500 other men, women, and children joined him. The ships also carried vital cargo and livestock they would need to establish their settlements.

The journey was very difficult. Eleven of the ships either turned back or did not survive the 750-mile journey through storms and large icebergs.

Those who reached Greenland faced more challenges. The region provided limited natural resources. There were few trees to provide wood for homes or boats. There was no iron for tools and weapons. The settlers had to trade with Norway and Iceland for many essentials. The best hunting—for food and trade items like walrus tusks—was hundreds of miles north of the settlements.

There were two main settlements. Eventually they would be home to over 2,000 people. Both were on the western edge of the island. Leif and his family lived in **Brattahlid**, one of the best locations. This was part of the "Eastern Settlement." The other was the "Western Settlement."

Archaeologists are scientists who use the remains from early people to learn how they lived. In Greenland, archeologists have uncovered the remains from some 400 farms in the Eastern Settlement and 80 more in the Western Settlement.

Like Vikings in Scandinavia and Iceland, Greenland settlers made good use of what was available. They built houses from

These ruins are believed to be of Erik the Red's house in Brattahlid on the western edge of Greenland.

sod. Dirt held together by the roots of grass was cut into bricks and used to build one-room, one-story homes.

Bits of fabric found at Greenland burial sites show that Vikings wore wool clothing, which may have been supplemented with animal skins. Men wore long pants covered by tunics. Often they wore a cloak over their other clothing, fastened at the collar by an elaborate brooch. Women wore brooches as well, which fastened a sort of apron over the shoulders of their long gowns. Some fifty different styles of brooches have been uncovered, many made of gold or silver.

Sometimes crafted of gold or silver, Viking brooches like these held their clothes together while revealing the social status of their owners.

While Leif Erikson's father helped develop the settlements and acted as chief of the island, the boy was separated from his family when he was eight. He was not being banished. He was just following a Viking tradition. Leif moved in with **Thyrker**, his father's German slave. Thyrker became like Leif's father. His job was to train Leif to be a good Viking.

As the oldest son of an important Viking chief, Leif learned how to be a leader. He trained in fighting with Viking weapons, like the double-edged sword and battle ax. He learned how to defend himself with a shield. There were also lessons on sailing

Das Langschwert war die typische Waffe des Kriegers in der Wikingerzeit. Prunkschwerter waren darüber hinaus Zeichen eines sozialen Ranges.

Although fairly simple in construction, the double-edged Viking sword could be a fearsome weapon.

and running a Viking crew. Besides skills for raiding and exploration, he learned how to read and write along with the history of his people.

Runes

To read and write, Vikings used the runic alphabet that first developed in Scandinavia around the year 100 CE. It had 24 letters, which were derived from letters from the Roman and Greek alphabets. Runes are sometimes called "futhark" after the first six runic letters (f-u-th-a-r-k), in the same way that the word "alphabet" comes from alpha and beta, the first two Greek letters.

The letters were very simple, consisting mainly of straight lines. The primary reason for this shape is that runes were often inscribed on boards made of wood, stone, or steel. Lines were much easier to inscribe than curves or other shapes.

Runic writing was meant to be permanent. It usually appears as brief inscriptions, such as a memorial for a dead warrior. These runic writings have been found across Europe. The runes were not used for longer writings. Instead the Vikings had oral traditions—stories were passed on by storytellers without being written down.

By 700, the simple runic alphabet had become even simpler when it was trimmed to 16 letters. Eventually runes were largely replaced by the Latin alphabet as more and more countries adopted Christianity.

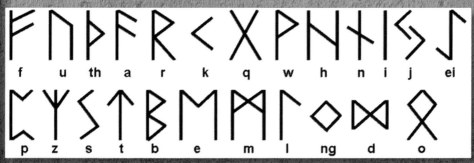

Called the "futhark" after its first six letters, the runic alphabet was brought to Iceland and Greenland from Scandinavia by the Vikings.

One of Reykjavik, Iceland's main landmarks, the Church Hallgrimskirkja features a statue of Leif Erikson designed by American Alexander Stirling Calder. The statue was donated by the United States in 1930 for the country's Millennial Festival.

Losing His Religion

King **Olaf Tryggvason** took his religion seriously. After being crowned king of Norway in 995, he destroyed Viking temples and built Christian churches. When a group of Vikings suggested the king needed to make a sacrifice to Thor, Olaf agreed. He told them they would be the sacrifice. The Vikings quickly became Christians.

Leif was probably still a teenager when he left Greenland for Norway, setting sail sometime around 999. He still hoped to visit the distant lands Bjarni Herjólfsson described. But although Leif often sailed with his father, Erik the Red did not think his son was ready for such a dangerous journey. By having his son visit King Olaf, Erik hoped to improve his island's trade with Norway. Erik's worries seemed justified when Leif's ship was blown off course. Instead of landing on Norway, Leif was forced to spend the summer in the Hebrides, a group of islands north of Scotland that were controlled by the Vikings. The

Based on a drawing by Norwegian historical painter Peter Nicolai Arbo (1831–1892), this illustration shows King Olaf Tryggvason's arrival in Norway. He soon made Christianity the state religion.

unexpected side trip turned out to be a blessing. It was here that he met his wife, **Thorgunna**. Soon she give birth to his first son, **Thorgils**.

In the fall he sailed to Norway and met King Olaf. *The Saga of Erik the Red* said that "the king formed an excellent opinion of him, and it appeared to him that Leif was a well-bred man."[1] Olaf asked Leif to preach Christianity in Greenland.

"Leif said that he was willing to undertake it," the saga went on, "but that, for himself, he considered that message a difficult one to proclaim in Greenland. But the king said that he knew no man who was better fitted for the work than he."[2]

Leif agreed. After Leif converted to Christianity, the king promised that he would carry good luck with him. This promise appeared to be proven when Leif rescued some stranded sailors on the return trip. That rescue provided his nickname of Leif the Lucky, by which he is still known today.

Leif arrived in Greenland with priests and plans for a Christian church. His mother, **Thjodhild**, embraced the religion, even overseeing the construction of a church in Brattahlid. Its ruins may have been the ones discovered in 1961 when a school was being built.

Soon the settlements in Greenland supported a dozen Christian churches. Many Vikings in the island converted. Leif's father refused.

After Leif Erikson's mother, Thjodhild, converted to Christianity she oversaw the construction of a church. This is a recreation of her simple Brattahlid church.

A·D·—·1000

Leif Erikson

DISCOVERER OF AMERICA

Leif Erikson commanded a ship while he was still in his teens. Ocean voyages were dangerous and unpredictable, but those who succeeded

often enjoyed untold wealth. He is believed to be the first European to set foot on North American shores.

By then the settlement was in trouble. In general, Vikings were self-sufficient. This means they produced everything they needed. They grew their own food and raised their own animals. They built their own homes and ships. Although they often traded with merchants for goods they could not produce, the Vikings did not depend on these trades.

In Europe, even in Iceland, anything the Vikings wanted could be taken during raids. Greenland was different. The island was too far from European shores to mount successful raids. Even if it was possible, the Viking ships were falling apart. There were not enough trees on the island to produce the wood to repair their boats and craft new ones.

Since he had first heard Bjarni Herjólfsson's stories of mysterious forested lands, Leif had always dreamed of traveling there. After he returned from Norway, Leif's father finally agreed to lead the trip.

Leif began planning the voyage. Traveling hundreds of miles across the storm-ravaged Atlantic Ocean was very dangerous. He needed a ship he could count on. Leif didn't just trust the accuracy of Bjarni Herjólfsson's stories. He also trusted his boat. Leif bought the same boat Herjólfsson had commanded when he saw the unknown lands.

They were ready to leave when Erik the Red fell from a horse. He injured his ankle in the fall. He knew it was a sign that he was not meant to go on the voyage. Leif would have to take over.

So sometime around 1001, Leif loaded Bjarni's boat with supplies and a crew of 35 men, some of whom had sailed with Bjarni. He also brought Thyrker. Then they set off into the unknown.

Viking Gods and Goddesses

Unlike the Christian, Jewish, and Islamic religions, Vikings worshipped more than one god. They had dozens of gods and goddesses. Vikings believed their gods were much like themselves—they got hungry, they slept, they even died. The difference was the gods lived much longer (few Vikings were around to celebrate their 40th birthday). The gods also had more power and ability.

Odin led the Viking gods. Vikings believed that Odin created their language and alphabet. Despite those achievements, Odin's son Thor—the god of war and/ or law—was more celebrated. During storms, Vikings said thunder was his voice, while lightning was caused when he flung his war hammer to the ground. Many Vikings like Leif's father, Erik Thorvaldson, and his grandfather Thorvald Aswaldson took Thor's name to honor the god. Today, two days of the week—Wednesday and Thursday—reflect the names of those two important gods.

Thor's Fight with the Giants by Mårten Eskil Winge (1825–1896)

The moment of a Viking's death was chosen by women called **Valkyries**, or "choosers of the slain." If Vikings died in battle, the Valkyries led them to **Valhalla** (the hall of the dead) where they enjoyed fighting battles all day and drinking mead all night.

In Boston, Massachusetts this statue of Leif Erikson peers out at shoppers visiting the Commonwealth Mall. Although it was once believed that the explorer reached the state's shores, today evidence suggests he never traveled south of Canada.

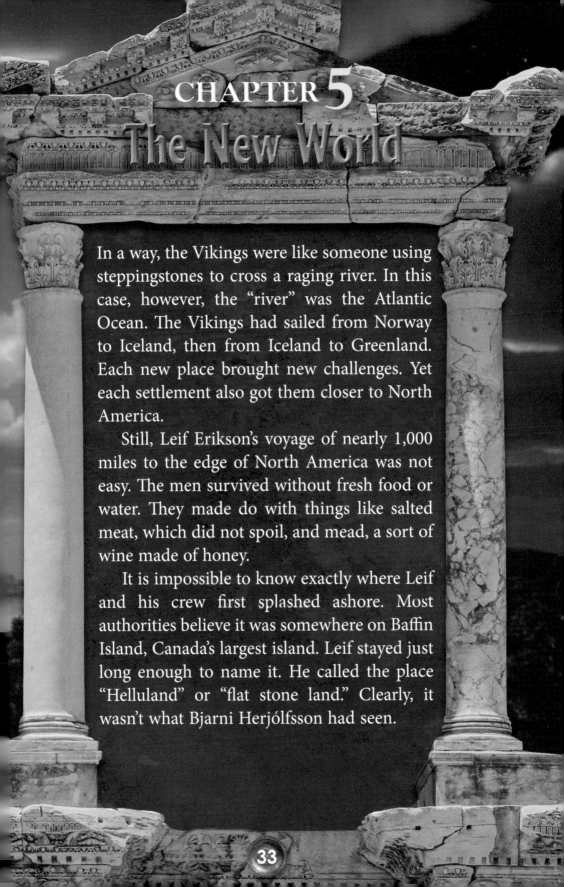

CHAPTER 5
The New World

In a way, the Vikings were like someone using steppingstones to cross a raging river. In this case, however, the "river" was the Atlantic Ocean. The Vikings had sailed from Norway to Iceland, then from Iceland to Greenland. Each new place brought new challenges. Yet each settlement also got them closer to North America.

Still, Leif Erikson's voyage of nearly 1,000 miles to the edge of North America was not easy. The men survived without fresh food or water. They made do with things like salted meat, which did not spoil, and mead, a sort of wine made of honey.

It is impossible to know exactly where Leif and his crew first splashed ashore. Most authorities believe it was somewhere on Baffin Island, Canada's largest island. Leif stayed just long enough to name it. He called the place "Helluland" or "flat stone land." Clearly, it wasn't what Bjarni Herjólfsson had seen.

After enduring a difficult voyage, Leif Erikson was rewarded with the New World, setting foot on the resource-rich land unexplored by Europeans.

Traveling south along the coast of North America, Leif reached an area that seemed to match Bjarni's description. It was flat and wooded, with the ocean waves lapping along a white sandy beach. Leif knew the vast stands of trees could support the Vikings' timber needs. He called it "Markland" or "forest land." It probably was somewhere on the coast of modern-day Labrador in Canada.

Leif was not done exploring. He continued further south, to the place where he and his men would camp for the winter. It became the first Viking settlement in North America, and in all likelihood was somewhere on the coast of present-day Newfoundland. Leif and his crew cut logs to bring home. They also built a large house and a shed to protect their ship. The men explored the area. One day, Thyrker came back, almost too excited to speak. He had found grapes. The men quickly turned it into wine. In Greenland, wine was both popular and as scarce as trees. As a result of this discovery, Leif called the new settlement "Vinland," or "the land where grapes grow."

After a long winter in North America, Leif Erikson returned to Greenland. Every available spot in the ship was packed with timber, and apparently they towed a small boat filled with grapes. He was welcomed home as a hero. He'd brought news of timber and wine, of new lands and new places to live. In turn, some momentous news was waiting for him. While he'd been away, his father had died. Leif Erikson was the new chief of Greenland. He never returned to North America. The last mention of him while he was still living was in 1019. He probably died in 1025 or perhaps a few years earlier.

His explorations changed the lives of his fellow Vikings. They made additional trips to the lands he had discovered, and even established a small settlement. Archaeologists uncovered evidence in the 1960s that as many as 75 people may have lived there. But the tribes of Native Americans who lived in eastern Canada considered the Vikings to be invaders. Despite their fighting ability, there were far too many Native Americans for

Just as Erik the Red had turned frigid Greenland into a Viking settlement, his son Leif Erikson led his men to build houses in hopes that "Vinland" would become a new home for his people.

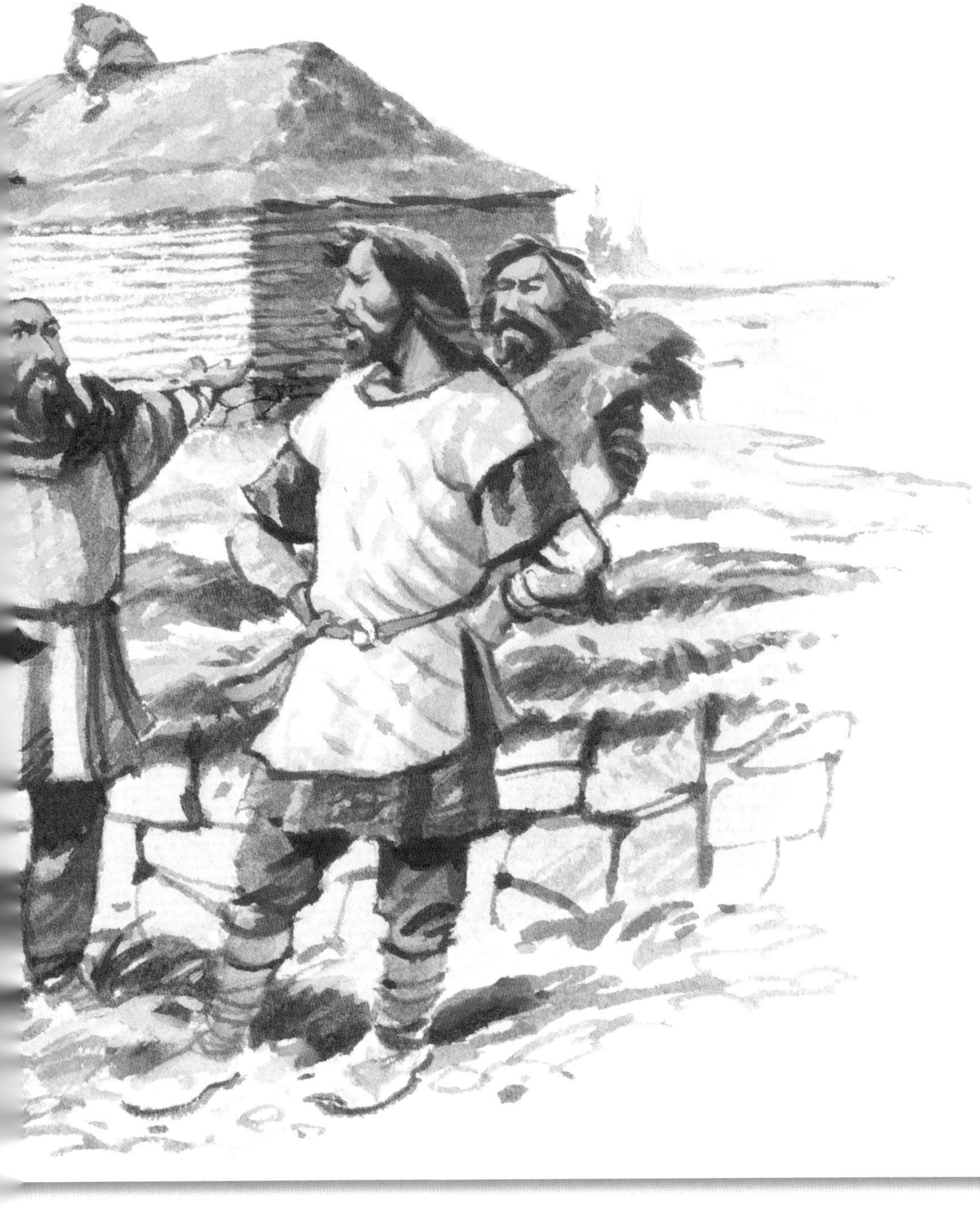

the Vikings to overcome. The settlement appears to have been abandoned after about 10 years from the time of its founding.

Despite the setback, the Vikings continued to make trading voyages to North America for centuries. But the slow chill of climate change made it difficult to farm or raise animals back home in Greenland. The Vikings finally abandoned the island in the early 1400s.

In a letter, Christopher Columbus said he visited Iceland in 1477 as part of the crew of a Portuguese ship. He learned about the Vikings and their explorations of the New World. Fifteen years later, he landed on an island near Florida and believed he had discovered a new world. Still, today Leif Erikson is regarded as the first European to set foot on North American shores.

His memory is honored in the United States by Leif Erikson Day, celebrated on October 9. The date isn't related to any specific event in Leif's life. Instead, it is the date in 1825 when the first ship carrying Norwegian immigrants arrived in New York.

On Leif Erikson Day in 2009, President Barack Obama proclaimed that "over a millennium ago, Leif Erikson—son of Iceland and grandson of Norway—arrived in North America and founded the settlement Vinland, located in modern-day Canada. Today, we celebrate his historic voyage and remember those who journeyed to America from far-away lands."[1] Leif Erikson Day comes a few days before Columbus Day. That is appropriate, because Leif Erikson discovered North America before Columbus.

Sagas

Much of what we know about the Vikings, Leif Erikson, and his father are due to long stories called sagas. Many of these stories were first written between 1100 and 1300, at least a hundred years after the events they described. Until then, the stories were passed down by word of mouth. Families developed sagas which made them look adventuresome or made rival families look weak.

Two of them recount the exploits of Leif Erikson. They are *The Greenlanders Saga* and *The Saga of Erik the Red*. They offer very different versions of how Leif Erikson reached North America. It is not possible to know which version is more accurate.

The first archeologists who studied the Vikings in Iceland, Greenland, and North America were guided by these sagas. Because so many ruins were discovered in places mentioned in the sagas, at first the archaeologists believed the sagas were accurate. Today they realize many of these descriptions are incorrect. For example, the clothing described in the sagas matches what was worn in 1200 instead of the time when Leif Erikson lived. Yet they fulfill a useful function in understanding Leif Erikson and the other heroic Vikings.

The Saga of Erik the Red was written a century or two after the Viking leader's death. Although many of its stories are inaccurate, some descriptions give insight into Viking life.

ca. 980   Leif Erikson is born in Iceland.

982   Leif's father, Erik Thorvaldson (Erik the Red) is banished from Iceland.

982–985   Erik the Red explores Greenland.

985   Between 500 and 1500 people, including Leif and his family, settle in Greenland. While lost at sea, Bjarni Herjólfsson spots the coast of what turns out to be North America.

999   Leif Erikson sails to Norway but is blown off course and lands in the Hebrides Islands, where he meets his wife, Thorgunna.

1000   After meeting Norway's King Olaf, Leif converts to Christianity; he returns to Greenland and spreads the religion across the island.

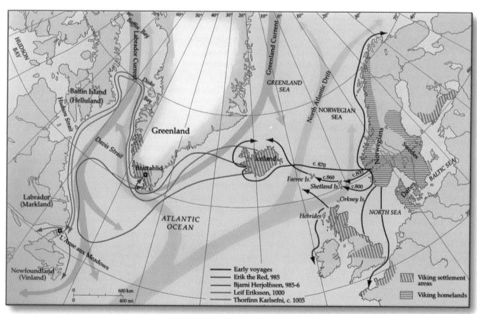

The map above shows the Vikings' journeys as they went to discover North America, about 500 years before Columbus found it. In 985, Erik the Red reached Greenland and his son, Leif Erikson eventually reached Newfoundland in about 1000.

1001	Leif sails to North America, building a settlement he calls Vinland.
1002	Leif returns to Greenland and becomes chief after the death of his father.
1019	Leif is mentioned in written records for the final time.
ca. 1025	Leif Erikson dies in Greenland.

TIMELINE

768	Charlemagne (Charles the Great) becomes king of France.
787	First Viking raid on England takes place.
793	Vikings attack monastery at Lindisfarne, marking the beginning of the Age of the Vikings.
841	Vikings establish a settlement at Dublin, Ireland.
865–879	The Great Viking Army invades England and stays for 14 years.
866	Vikings capture York and kill King Edmund of East Anglia.
878	Some 300 Viking ships attack the forces of King Alfred of Wessex, but lose the battle.
885	Vikings besiege Paris but withdraw the following year.
900	Gunnbjorn Ulfsson spots islands off the coast of Greenland and names them Gunnbjorn's skerries.
930	The first Althing meets in Iceland.

935	Harold Bluetooth becomes first Christian king of Denmark.
963	First mention of London Bridge spanning the Thames River in England.
995	King Olaf Tryggvason is crowned King of Norway.
1000	Olaf dies in battle.
1030	First documented mention of Vienna, which becomes one of the most important cities in Europe.
1040	Macbeth becomes king of Scotland; he later becomes the subject of one of William Shakespeare's most famous plays.
1066	William the Conquerer, who is related to the Vikings, invades England.
1096	The Crusades, the attempts of Christians to regain the Holy Land from Muslims, begin; they last for several centuries.
1100	The end of the Viking Age.
1408	A marriage on Greenland is the final written record of Viking settlements there.

Leif Erikson Monument,
Humbolt Park,
Chicago, Illinois

Chapter 1: Land of Trees
1. Will Durant, *The Story of Civilization, Part IV: The Age of Faith.* (New York: Simon and Schuster, 1950), p. 506.
2. R.A. Hall, *The World of the Vikings.* (New York: Thames & Hudson, 2007), p. 72.

Chapter 2: Punishing Voices
1. Robert Ferguson, *The Vikings: A History.* (New York, Viking, 2009), p. 280.
2. J. Sephton (translator), *The Saga of Erik the Red*, Chapter 2. Icelandic Saga Database. http://sagadb.org/eiriks_saga_rauda.en

Chapter 3: Losing His Religion
1. J. Sephton (translator), *The Saga of Erik the Red*, Chapter 5. Icelandic Saga Database. http://sagadb.org/eiriks_saga_rauda.en
2. Ibid.

Chapter 5: The New World
1. Leif Erikson Day, 2009—By the President of the United States of America: A Proclamation. http://www.whitehouse.gov/the-press-office/presidential-proclamation-leif-erikson-day

This statue of Leif Erikson is in Cleveland, Ohio. The caption reads:
LEIF ERIKSON VIKING EXPLORER
The first European to establish a settlement on the North American continent, 1000–1003 A.D. Dedicated August 25, 2001 by the Scandinavian Community of Northeast Ohio.

Books

Glaser, Jason. *Leif Eriksson*. Mankato, Minnesota: Capstone Press, 2005.

Huey, Lois Miner. *American Archaeology Uncovers the Vikings*. Tarrytown, New York: Marshall Cavendish Benchmark, 2010.

Klingel, Cynthia Fitterer and Robert B. Noyed. *Leif Eriksson: Norwegian Explorer*. Chanhassen, Minnesota: Child's World, 2003.

Knudsen, Shannon and Mark Oldroyd. *Leif Eriksson*. Minneapolis, Minnesota: Carolrhoda Books, 2005.

Lassieur, Allison, Ron Frenz, and Charles Barnett. *Lords of the Sea: the Vikings Explore the North Atlantic*. Mankato, Minnesota: Capstone Press, 2006.

Langley, Andrew, David Antram, and David Salariya. *You Wouldn't Want to be a Viking Explorer: Voyages You'd Rather Not Make*. New York: Franklin Watts, 2001.

Works Consulted

Durant, Will. *The Story of Civilization, Part IV: The Age of Faith*. New York: Simon and Schuster, 1950.

Ferguson, Robert. *The Vikings: A History*. New York: Viking, 2009.

Fitzburgh, William and Elizabeth Ward, ed. *Vikings: The North Atlantic Saga*. Washington: Smithsonian Press, 2000.

Hall, R. A. "Raiders and Invaders: Targets and Tactics," *The World of the Vikings*. New York: Thames & Hudson, 2007.

DVD

Harl, Kenneth W. "Western Voyages to Greenland and Vinland," *The Vikings*. Chantilly, Virginia: The Great Courses, 2005.

Periodicals

Brown, Dale M. "The Fate of Greenland's Vikings." *Archaeology*, February 2000. http://www.archaeology.org/online/features/greenland/index.html

Catto, Susan. "Vikings Return to Newfoundland." *New York Times*, May 28, 2000. http://www.nytimes.com/2000/05/28/travel/travel-advisory-vikings-return-to-newfoundland.html

Richardson, Sarah. "Vanished Vikings." *Discover*, March 2000. http://discovermagazine.com/2000/mar/featvanished#.USY-pGe6gcs

Tierney, John. "After Ocean Trip, Leif's Descendant Says Vikings Were Here." *New York Times*, October 6, 2000. http://www.nytimes.com/2000/10/06/nyregion/the-big-city-after-ocean-trip-leif-s-descendant-says-vikings-were-here.html

On the Internet

"Ancient History: Vikings," BBC History http://www.bbc.co.uk/history/ancient/vikings/

Budardalur, Iceland Travel Guide http://www.nat.is/travelguideeng/budardalur.htm

"Lunchbreak: Midnight Sun, Iceland," Joe Capra's time lapse video of a summer's day in Iceland when the sun never sets. *The Washington Post*, October 19, 2011. http://www.washingtonpost.com/blogs/ezra-klein/post/lunchbreak-midnight-sun-iceland/2011/10/19/gIQAaPrqxL_blog.html

Sanderson, Nicole. "Write Your Name in Runes." The Vikings, NOVA. http://www.pbs.org/wgbh/nova/ancient/write-your-name-in-runes.html

Sephton, J. (translator). *The Saga of Erik the Red*. The Icelandic Saga Database. http://sagadb.org/eiriks_saga_rauda.en

Aethelred (ETH-uhl-red)

Bjarni Herjólfsson (BEE-yar-nee HER-olf-suhn)

Brattahlid (BRAH-tah-leehd)

Budardalur (BOO-dar-dahl-ehr)

Eyjolf (EHY-yohlf)

Faeroes (FAIR-ohs)

Gunnbjorn Ulfsson (GUHN-bee-yawrn UHLF-suhn)

Hallgrimskirkja (hatl-KREAMS-kyir-kah)

Hebrides (HEB-ri-deez)

Hrafn (RAHF-ihn)

knorr (NOR)

Leif (LAYF)

Lindisfarne (LIN-duhs-fahrn)

Olaf Tryggvason (OH-lihf trig-VAH-suhn)

Reykjavik (ray-KAH-veek)

Snæbjörn Galti (SNAY-bee-yawrn GAHL-tee)

Thjodhild (THEE-yoh-hild)

Thorgils (THOR-gihls)

Thorgunna (THOR-guhn-nah)

Thorvald Aswaldson (thar-VALD as-WALD-suhn)

Thorvaldson (thar-VALD-suhn)

Thyrker (THEER-kehr)

Valhalla (val-HAL-uh)

Valkyrie (val-KEER-ee)

arable (AIR-uh-buhl)—Capable of being farmed.

archaeologists (ahr-kee-AHL-uh-jists)—Scientists who study the past by uncovering ruins and other material from ancient civilizations.

draft (DRAFT)—Distance between a vessel's waterline and the bottom of its keel.

fjords (fee-YORDZ)—Narrow inlets of the sea that lie between steep cliffs.

glacier (GLAY-shur)—A large body of ice slowly moving down a slope or valley.

keel (KEEL)—Principal structural element of a vessel, which runs lengthwise along its centerline from front to back and to which the framing is attached.

latitude (LAT-ih-tood)—Angular distance north or south of the equator; the North Pole is 90 degrees North Latitude and a point midway between the North Pole and the equator would be 45 degrees North Latitude.

ruins (ROO-ins)—What remains of villages or towns after being destroyed by time.

tunics (TOO-niks)—Loose-fitting jackets which reach the wearer's knees.